GRACE

Maurice Fullard Smith

GRACE

with illustrations by
Nick Butterworth

Marshall Pickering is an Imprint of
HarperCollins*Religious*
Part of HarperCollins*Publishers*
77-85 Fulham Palace Road, London W6 8JB

First published in Great Britain in 1999 by Marshall Pickering

1 3 5 7 9 10 8 6 4 2

Text copyright © 1999 Maurice Fullard Smith
Illustrations copyright © 1999 Nick Butterworth

Maurice Fullard Smith and Nick Butterworth assert the moral right to be identified as
the author and illustrator of this work.

A catalogue record for this book is
available from the British Library.

ISBN 0 551 03184 0

Printed and bound in Great Britain by
Woolnough Bookbinding Ltd, Irthlingborough, Northamptonshire

So many people have urged me to write a book about grace. I have never responded to the idea of a book. But small booklets can work wonders and two in particular have been a great help to me.

I must have read The Exchanged Life *by Hudson Taylor a hundred times. I knew there was something wonderful in that little booklet, but it was a long time before the truth dawned. The other booklet was by Norman Grubb, who eventually became a friend. He wrote* The Key to Everything *and it cost ninepence!*

I am writing for those people in the church who are disappointed with their efforts to live 'the Christian life', for those who feel condemned. I would also love to whet the appetite of those who have steered clear of anything to do with Christianity because it seems so full of demanding rules and regulations.

My theme is very simple. God is a God of grace.

Let me make clear that an experience of that grace may not lead others to the same place as me. Nor do I think that to be where I am is to have 'arrived'. I believe grace sets us free to become ourselves. We may pursue quite different lifestyles and explore very different ways of expressing our freedom. The quest for accuracy of doctrine or purity of religious expression has never interested me. Life is so much more than that.

Surely we will be learning to live until our dying day.

Maurice Fullard Smith

GRACE The enjoyment of forgiveness

Early on in my adult life, I discovered that God is gracious and has a disposition to forgive. I found it everywhere, clearly in the heart of Jesus in His dealings with adulterers and criminals, and especially with me, one who had committed the biggest, and perhaps the only real sin, from which all other failings spring: independence from God, the determination to run my own show.

It is more than thirty years since I began to speak about grace. One of the first occasions was at a house church in Welwyn Garden City. When I left, they hung a banner across the lounge wall proclaiming: 'Grace is the enjoyment of Forgiveness'. I shall never forget, because another visiting speaker saw the banner and commented, 'Grace is much more than that!' And so it is, but I didn't know that at the time. I had been speaking about what was real in my own experience.

If you have fallen out with someone dear to you and you make up, have you noticed that the atmosphere is much sweeter afterwards than it was before anything went wrong? Pure enjoyment fills the air. All is right again. Even the tears seem worth the reward. That is how it is when forgiveness has been extended, when grace has been at work. Our hearts burn within us. We can *feel* the change.

Many say that we must not live on feelings alone. Of course, that is true, but I find myself in agreement with John Wesley who exclaimed, 'That accursed doctrine of faith without feelings!' We may not all show our feelings to the same degree, but our feelings are there as evidence of what we experience.

In the final analysis, grace cannot be taught. Grace must be experienced, and can only become a revelation to those who know they need it. Sadly, to others, grace remains a matter of doctrine or information. There is no thrill of enjoyment, no knowledge of God's heart with a disposition to forgive.

GRACE Love in action

If I say I love you but continually act ungraciously towards you, then I guess you have a right to question the depth of my love. Actions speak louder than words.

Grace is not a word we use much today. Perhaps the most common use is when we talk about being given 'a period of grace'. We cannot pay up in the required time and so someone decrees we do not have to pay our dues right away. We are let off. And I suppose that helps us understand grace a little more.

God took action and sent His son into the world to reveal the Father's heart to us. God knows we are way behind with our payments, with our ability to be all that

is desirable towards our fellow man, and He takes action. We cannot pay up and He lets us off. Again and again and again. Not just until we can pay; we owe nothing because the debt is completely cancelled.

Christianity is so often portrayed as a set of laws or rules that should govern our behaviour. The law (to use a biblical term) sets a standard of behaviour and seems to demand that we do something for God. But grace means God does something for us. That is it in a nutshell. God does something and He does it entirely on His own initiative. He loves us, forgives us and accepts us exactly as we are.

This has nothing to do with anything we have done for Him. It has nothing to do with having earned anything or with getting what we deserve. In fact I am often very grateful I do not get what I deserve!

The classic definition of grace is 'free unmerited favour', and that is exactly what we receive. Not surprisingly, this invokes love in return from us, both towards God and our fellow man. When we experience God's grace, love wells up in spite of our many unanswered questions and all the terrible suffering we see in the world and the pain we personally bear. We begin to live with a paradox.

Strangely enough, in the end, God *is* paid back, but not out of duty or by coercion. It is a glorious side effect of His own unconditional act of love. There are no strings attached.

GRACE It's unilateral

G race is entirely one way. It is flowing all the time. God is not sitting, high and mighty, on a throne of judgement waiting for us to say we are sorry before He steps down to sit upon a lower throne of grace. Mercy has already overcome judgement.

My wife Eileen and I have been married for fifty years, but we still have our ups and downs. I remember that once I wanted her to admit she had been wrong about something and I said, 'All you have to do is say you are sorry and I will forgive you!'

The truth is that such an attitude makes it virtually impossible to apologize even if we know we are wrong.

But if we know we are already forgiven and will walk straight into the arms of forgiveness when we turn around, it all becomes so much easier.

Our good news is not that we can be forgiven, but that we are forgiven.

There is a remarkable spin-off from knowing we are not being continually judged by God, continually under the spotlight. We find we are not always judging ourselves

and we are not bothered by what others think of us either. What a relief! And that is not all; when we stop judging ourselves, we find that we stop passing judgement on others and become more forgiving.

A friend sent me this poem (I would love to know who wrote it) which spoke volumes to me about judgement:

> *I dreamed death came the other night*
> *And heaven's gate swung wide;*
> *An angel with a halo bright*
> *Ushered me inside.*
> *And there, to my astonishment*
> *Stood folk I'd judged and labelled*
> *As 'quite unfit', of 'little worth'*
> *And 'spiritually disabled'.*
> *Indignant words rose to my lips,*
> *But never were set free,*
> *For every face showed stunned surprise,*
> *Not one expected me!*

GRACE Learned through experience

I used to be very intolerant of outrageous dressers –
skinheads, punks and the like. And people who
scrawled messages on walls were the lowest form of
human life to me. I could never understand such mindless
behaviour. I would say, 'They ought to be shot!' I now
realize that I was actually scared of these non-conformists.

Since army days I have enjoyed running. One Saturday
morning, now aged fifty-plus and with impressive running
gear adorning my less than impressive body, I was slumped
at my desk deterred from leaving home. Someone in my
family was suffering deeply and I had no answer. Frankly,
I had had more than I could bear and was beginning to

fragment. I vaguely hoped the release of adrenalin whilst pounding the pavements would be some help.

Gradually, a strange feeling crept over me: it was the desire for a mammoth piece of chalk and a huge lavatory wall! I just longed to scrawl horrible messages to express my frustration with the world, the system, my lack of money to buy first-class medical treatment for my family. Everything.

I was appalled. I'd never thought myself capable of such base desires. Eventually I came to terms with the feeling and realized yet again that I am no better than anyone else.

In this mood, I jogged out of my gate to start my strenuous training run. As I touched the pavement I was startled to see half a dozen burly skinheads within a few feet of me. I looked at them and smiled. Yes me! I cannot analyse it fully, but I guess I had accepted that we were all of the same stuff. I felt I understood these lads, a little of their frustration, and found I was looking beyond their appearance.

They all formed up in line and ran close behind me across the road with their boots making a loud clatter in my ears, but I found I was not scared.

As I continued to smile and resisted a sprint, they began to smile back at me and one of them said, 'You're alright mate!' and they peeled off back across the road. I had been gracious to those I would previously have despised and discovered they were actually a likeable bunch!

It had been an encounter that helped change my life a little more. It helped me ease a little further into accepting everyone without passing judgement.

GRACE A tone of voice

I was exasperated by the seeming superiority and hypocrisy I could see in some of the officers in a church where I was invited to preach. So I decided to let them have some very strong words from the pulpit.

I took as my text, 'You scribes and Pharisees, you blind guides . . . which strain at a gnat and swallow a camel!' It went down like a lead balloon. I convinced nobody and achieved nothing.

Later that night I poured out my complaint to God: 'But Jesus used those very words!' I groaned through my misery. My world stood still as an inaudible voice inside me seemed to whisper, 'Yes son, but He never used that tone of voice. He loved the scribes and Pharisees and would have gathered them, if only they had let Him.'

I learned that night that God speaks in tones of love even when He is angry. I had been intolerant and judgemental, not speaking from a caring heart. I wonder now, how Jesus was feeling inside as He took a whip to the profiteers in the temple? Maybe one day I shall know.

I am convinced we just cannot dig words out of the Bible and use them to hit out at others. We are called to love, and love always has another's best interest at heart. That day saw the beginning of the end for my own

self-righteous indignation. I would like to learn the easy way for a change, but people with my temperament seldom do.

Sometimes, it is hard to discern a tone of voice from the written page. But if we know well the heart of the one writing the words, it becomes much easier. When we are convinced that God never says or does anything except from a motive of love, we are better equipped to hear the heart behind the words.

GRACE It's not scary

I was travelling in the USA and speaking on my favourite theme, that of living by grace. Leaving things to God. Living from deep within, doing what you deep-down want to do. Some of my hearers seemed to find the idea unsettling.

'Man, that's scary!' said one person, feeling like so many that we cannot and should not trust ourselves. One man even confessed, 'If I did that I would be straight off into an orgy!'

All of this reveals a lack of understanding of how radical a true encounter with God is. Such an encounter reaches right into our hearts and replaces base desires

with an urge to love and do good. Once we have seen the light shining in the face of 'That Man', as I love to call Jesus, we are never the same again. Our identity crisis is on the way to being resolved.

We shall make mistakes, perhaps dreadful mistakes, but there will be a point of recall. Like an ancient hymn writer we shall say:

What has stripped the seeming beauty
From the idols of the earth?
Not a sense of right or duty
But the sight of peerless worth.

It is the sight of peerless worth, the sight of Him who was 'full of grace and reality', that can turn the heavy struggle of duty into a 'light burden' and an 'easy yoke'.

Once we have seen that by our own efforts the Christian life is not difficult to live, but quite impossible, then we can turn to the One who is 'the light that lights every man who comes into the world' and begin to live from within: what my friend and Christian philosopher Norman Grubb used to call 'leaning inwards'.

It is not scary at all. It is perfectly safe to trust God as we learn to live from His life inside us, from that grace springing up from within.

GRACE It can rock the boat

Many years ago I went with a young singer friend of mine to a church in the north of England. There were about five hundred people present and by the time we had finished speaking and singing the congregation was obviously moved.

The leader of the church actually embraced me on the platform and said, 'We've never heard anything like it.' The 'it' was our story of grace. People saw that the life inside them was reliable and trustworthy. They could trust their innermost being.

To celebrate the evening, Dave the singer and I were invited back for a fish-and-chip supper with the leaders.

The enthusiasm continued as we talked and ate together.

That is, until one bright young man asked, 'Suppose the congregation don't want to tithe?' (that is to give a tenth of their income to the church). Now we were getting down to the nitty-gritty! I replied that I did not think that God would want money that people did not really want to give. There was a stunned silence.

At last someone exploded, 'But we have a new building to pay for! We owe £100,000 – and we also have six men in full-time service who have to be paid!'

... and so there are two things to remember... Firstly, you should feel free to give as MUCH – or as little as you wish. And secondly, £12.47p from each member would clear the overdraft.

I simply said that God was trustworthy and if He wanted the building to be paid for and all those men financially supported by the church, then He would see that the money came in. If not, they could dispose of the building, repay the bank and the men could look for normal jobs. As usual I could not see the problem. I am renowned for that. But they could certainly see difficulties ahead and most of their faces registered stern disapproval. The excitement and the blessing of an hour ago had gone.

I was saddened to see the new-found joy turn back to heaviness of heart. Grace most certainly takes a lot of the strain out of living, but not if we are determined to forge ahead with our own plans regardless of the voice of God springing up within us.

GRACE It can be violent

Violent grace may sound like a contradiction in terms. But, when patience, invocation, and gentle insights fail to produce results, we sometimes find cruel events produce what gentler methods cannot.

I am not greatly qualified to expound on the purpose of suffering, but I am sure that so often the pain we bear is a rudder which guides our ship into the harbour of a deeper experience with God. It never seems so at the time, but over and over again I have found that God meets me in an extreme situation. As Jacob records, 'the gate of heaven is a dreadful place'. Perhaps I am not ready to hear until all my hectic activity is stilled. I do not like it and often tell God so. But He seems able to cope quite easily with my tantrums.

I believe it was a Scottish archbishop who said, 'Oh that men would vent their anger into the bosom of the Lord who is well able to bear it!' My language with God

is not so gentlemanly, I am afraid. When under intolerable pressure I tend to throw all my exasperating trials at Him: 'I can't cope with this! You'll have to deal with it! I see no way out!' . . . and worse.

The Old Testament exhorts us to 'cast our burdens on the Lord' and God is well able to cope, however clumsily we throw them in his direction. He is unshockable.

Sometimes, after having off-loaded our burdens on to God, we are tempted to believe we have taken them back on board again. But thankfully the years have taught me better. I do not take them back. They just come back. So I tell God that I gave them to Him and now He has to take responsibility for them. They are His problem. I cannot spend my whole life repeatedly throwing the same things at Him. So now I trust God to keep what I have committed to Him and ignore any returning feelings or worries. I do not worry that I worry! It is a great way to live.

I am no stoic and have a very low pain threshold. I have wept more than my share of midnight tears. I can be found shouting, 'It's too much!' again and again. And would you believe it? Peace comes . . . but eventually; I just cannot hurry this business along.

GRACE It's not cheap

S ome religious people want to earn God's acceptance
by serving others, by praying more, by faithful church
attendance or by studying the Bible. Or whatever. To such
people the message of unmerited acceptance seems utterly
outrageous and offensive. They cry out that we are offering
'cheap grace'. But it is not cheap. It is absolutely free.

Strangely enough, although grace is free, it does cost us
everything before we can ever enjoy it. Consenting that
without God's grace we can do nothing to qualify for His
acceptance is the most costly thing of all to many would-be
Christians. This is surely what Jesus meant by 'losing your
life to gain it'. He was not speaking of a life full of overtly

sacrificial acts, but giving up that independence which keeps us from all blessing. We are beholden to mercy alone, beneficiaries of grace. Even though this may be a very costly condition for many, what a wonderful offer it is to those who have longed for acceptance, to those who cannot make the grade under their own steam.

This dependence is not a one-off, it is a lifetime condition. Once into dependence upon God, it is not difficult to live our daily lives. We are no longer dogged by decisions between right and wrong. We are no longer living as if on a tightrope, where at any moment, if we put a foot wrong, we may plummet to destruction.

In fact, we cannot go ultimately wrong now that we are trusting God. We may well 'reap what we sow' at times, but all will come out right in the end. Not only are our problems God's problem, but *we* are God's problem. We are in God's hands now and we can live for the rest of our lives free from the crippling anxiety of not quite knowing how best to please Him.

'Too easy, too cheap – we must play our part!' insist many and they never experience the wonder of it all.

As the famous Christian teacher Dr Martin Lloyd-Jones once said: 'Any man who preaches the true grace of God is bound to be called antinomian (against the law)', and I am sure he was right.

But however much we consent that biblical injunctions and exhortations are good, the fact is, we just do not have the power to keep them. The apostle Paul, no doubt, got the blame for a lot of excesses as some used his 'glorious gospel of the grace of God' as an excuse to indulge their lusts, but that never prevented him sharing what he knew. The news was too good to keep to himself.

GRACE It's enabling

When we know we can do nothing, we begin to hear the whisper that we can do everything. Not all at once, perhaps. Life is a marathon, not a sprint. A crisis may well bring us to a revelation of the truth, but life is not all crisis, it is a process as well. We do not spend the whole time on the mountain-tops in everyday life. There are also valleys and plains in life's journey.

Although I have intimated that it is usually a crisis that brings us in real need to experience grace first-hand, I will not make a rule of that, for some are already fully aware of their inability to make the grade on their own. They need no such crisis.

Let me share an example from my own experience. I have always been tempted by the opposite sex in spite of loving my wife and wanting to remain faithful to her all my life. Thankfully, I do not confuse the temptation with actually doing something wrong.

When I leave for a long trip, Eileen does not tell me to be good, to be faithful, to put her photograph by the bed at night and not to talk to pretty women. Over the years, as she has waved goodbye to me, her attitude has seemed to say, 'I hope you are faithful to me. But whether you are or not, I will still love you.' That is true love in action.

There is power in such an attitude.

In his translation of the New Testament, Canon J.B. Phillips uncovers a beautiful truth. The apostle Paul has been saying, 'The more sin abounds, the more grace abounds,' and he follows this by saying, 'Shall we sin, then, to experience more grace?' The Authorized Version of the Bible answers this question with, 'God forbid.' But J.B. Phillips puts it this way: 'What a ghastly thought!'

And so it is, to any who have experienced the persistent love of God through Jesus Christ. Grace enables us to overcome temptations and fulfil our heart's desires. There is nothing for us to boast about. To quote Paul the apostle once again, we have been 'kept by the power of God'.

GRACE A poem

Jesus you have kept your precious promise,
You never left me, even for an hour.
You lived within and knew my deepest longing,
Loved me still when all my dreams turned sour.

Yet when in pride I sought to earn that loving,
Your face was sad, and dark clouds came between;
How quickly then the bright flame dwindled
And the inner light grew dim.

Then, when all my days were filled with fruitless seeking
For that which you alone in grace can give;
I ran into your arms – empty, weeping,
And with a gentle push you whispered:
Go and live.

Shirley Wing

GRACE It meets us where we are

We were late for a wedding and I cannot stand being late. We were also lost. Conveniently there were two old fellows standing on the pavement outside a pub, so I swung the car across the road and wound down the window.

I asked my way to our destination. After what seemed like an age, one of them declared, 'Sorry mate, you can't get there from 'ere!'

As we drove on, my annoyance turned to pondering the absurd statement. How impossible to start anywhere other than where we are! And if I know that, then it is a pretty good assumption that God does too.

How angry I still become when I hear teachers and preachers alike telling people how to experience grace; what they need to do, or even where they need to go. There are so many 'how to' books telling us which conference we need to attend, which is the only church we should join, and giving us a thousand other conditions to fulfil.

For most people, I have found it is time to be still, just where we are, and realize the grace of God. Where we are is where God can find us. Where else? For all his omnipresence, even God cannot meet us where we are not. We have to do nothing and go nowhere to receive the grace of God.

I am so thankful to be able to say, 'You *can* get there from here!'

GRACE It needs the right soil

There is no overt act which we can perform to make God's grace magically become real to us. However, there is a condition that often seems to be at the heart of such a discovery.

I am talking about honesty. Being real. Not pretending, but being ourselves, however unacceptable we might feel we are. At some time we have to let it all hang out and be truthful about what we think about something. Or someone. Or even about ourselves.

Being unreal and untruthful means we push down our feelings. Over a period of time, by failing to express ourselves openly, pretending and being nice on the

surface, things start to go wrong deep inside us. Bitterness can take a hold. We all know that bitter people can affect everyone with whom they come into contact.

None of us is naturally the required ground for the revelation of God's grace, but Jesus is reported to have said, 'Good and honest ground brings forth fruit one hundred fold.'

I am not advocating that we go around deliberately offending people, but that we stop pretending; that in genuine weakness we seek to be truthful. If we fail to express our true feelings, but always pretend and cover up our annoyances and even prejudices, we shall fail to receive grace . . . because there is apparently nothing we need help with. Some people appear never to be themselves, always acting, always wearing a mask. We can dare to come out of hiding, in the knowledge that God knows all about us and loves us as we are.

GRACE You are alright as you are

I know of no more liberating news than this. We just cannot go on forever trying to improve ourselves. It is a completely fruitless task. Even if we succeed, we would only end up exchanging our previous bad habits for a kind of smug self-righteousness.

I like to tell of the time I was speaking to a small audience in New Jersey, while just a few miles away, the prophet Joel was performing to a vast crowd at a baseball stadium. Billy Joel that is. He no doubt sang his great hit song which includes these words: *'Don't go changing, trying to please me. I love you just the way you are.'* There is such a shaft of divine light in those magnificent words.

I am persuaded that is exactly how God feels about us. Any changes that have to be made to our performance come from His initiative and His power at work within us. These changes are often achieved slowly. It is what the Bible refers to as 'being changed from one degree of glory to another'. Some impatient people may want us to change one hundred and eighty degrees at a time, but we

cannot do it. They will just have to wait, for God is not done with us yet and as I keep repeating, God is not in a hurry.

It is heartbreaking to see so many who are ill today because of performance orientation. Perfectionism is rife. Constant success is a very hard taskmaster. We live in a foolish generation.

So I beg you, hear the good news: do not try to change in order to please God and everyone else, you are loved as you are. Please do not be hard on yourself. Start to love yourself, for you are totally acceptable whatever your current performance or your past behaviour.

Breathe a sigh of relief as you take such acceptance down inside you. Breathe that air all the time, and leave any alteration to your performance in God's good hands.

GRACE Reveals God's hobby

I t is many years ago now that I decided to embark upon a week-long fast. Some prominent Christian leaders had been speaking of the benefits of long-term fasting and as someone with aspirations to be the next John Wesley, I couldn't afford to miss a trick.

I declared that I would take no solid food for a week. But the plan backfired. On Day One, I went down with agonising pains in unmentionable places. My best friend, who had heard of my plight, called round to cheer me up. 'Oh my goodness,' he exclaimed, 'you look terrible!'

The next visitor was my neighbour, who was taking redirected phone calls for me. 'Guess what,' he said. 'I've just had a call from a Black Magic circle. They say they have procured your death!' As I said, my efforts were not encouraging.

The pain got worse. Finally, at my lowest point, I swore – for the first time in years of pious living – and told God just what he could do with his 'high calling'. If this was my reward for dedication, then I wanted no more.

Stoically, I refused medical help, feeling that this would mean I was not trusting God. But by Day Six, I had wilted completely. I bleated out my complaint to God in more penitent terms.

'I've failed, Lord! Other men seem to be able to press on through, but they're made of sterner stuff. Under pressure, I swore at you and I gave up. I won't persevere with my ministry. I'm a failure.'

It was then, I experienced again, one of those rare, precious moments in life when the world seems to stand still. Whether or not the voice was audible, I will not say with certainty. But I *am* certain of what that still, small, voice said. 'Don't worry, Maurice, You'll be OK. You have discovered my hobby. *I collect failures.*'

Well, what do you know? God is not looking for great heroes, but weak people, through whom he can pour his strength.

The next morning, I was due to speak at Cambridge University. I got out of bed with the pain gone, but the weakness remaining. I was nervous. Yet I know I have never spoken with more authority.

Many years later as I told this story to a small conference, I concluded by saying, '. . .mind you, I'm not *trying* to fail.' It was then that someone at the back whispered, loud enough for every one to hear, 'Are you sure?'

Well, yes, I am sure. But I'm more wonderfully sure that not only is it alright to fail now and again, it's actually alright to be a failure. We'll be collected.

GRACE A final thought

We have read something of what grace is and what it can do, and no doubt 'grace is much more than that', as the preacher commented in my very first chapter. If what I have written seems right, but still somehow it eludes you, then never mind. Very often, it is when we give up trying to possess the truth that it dawns upon us. If we stand still, the butterfly may well land on our shoulder.

Truth is never just an academic or intellectual matter, but an encounter with God Himself. Somehow, when light comes, we are not just in possession of more information, but we know something more of God.

One young man wrote to me and asked how he could give up trying to get inner light on these matters. He was now *trying* to give up! The secret is not to try, but to trust. However, some of us will not let go until we cannot hang on any longer. The truth is, as I have said, we are alright wherever we are. I had to tell the young man that maybe he needed to give up giving up. Just be.

If you still feel you have to struggle on to receive more insight, then that is fine too, for you will probably, like me, finally exhaust yourself into rest. You can do no more and you then have to cease from your own efforts and leave things to God. Some of us learn no other way. Mercifully, God looks at the heart while all this struggling is going on. We are all different and He relates to us as the individuals that we are.

Some may have to go over the same ground many times, as I did with Hudson Taylor's *The Exchanged Life*, before the penny will drop. Maybe then, maybe days, months or years later, the mystery will unfold. No matter, for we cannot force the pace. There is a time for everything.

I wish you well. My fervent hope is not that you will come to understand the principles of grace more, but that you will find God in all around you, most especially within yourself, and so relax into your true identity. For in finding Him, we find ourselves and go on doing so.